HOORAY FOR MAIL CARRIERS!

by Tessa Kenan

BUMBA BOOKS™

LERNER PUBLICATIONS ◆ MINNEAPOLIS

Note to Educators:

Throughout this book, you'll find critical thinking questions. These can be used to engage young readers in thinking critically about the topic and in using the text and photos to do so.

Lerner Publications Company
A division of Lerner Publishing Group, Inc.
241 First Avenue North
Minneapolis, MN 55401 USA

For reading levels and more information, look up this title at www.lernerbooks.com.

Library of Congress Cataloging-in-Publication Data

The Cataloging-in-Publication Data for *Hooray for Mail Carriers!* is on file at the Library of Congress.
ISBN 978-1-5124-3354-8 (lib. bdg.)
ISBN 978-1-5124-5554-0 (pbk.)
ISBN 978-1-5124-5036-1 (EB pdf)

Manufactured in the United States of America
1 — CG — 7/15/17

Expand learning beyond the printed book. Download free, complementary educational resources for this book from our website, www.lernerresource.com.

Table of
Contents

Mail Carriers Bring Us Mail

Mail carriers work in our communities.

They bring us our mail.

Mail carriers work for the post office.

They bring us the mail people send.

Mail can be letters or packages.

What might a letter say?

Their days start at the post office.

The mail carriers pick up the mail.

They sort it into boxes.

Why do you think mail is sorted?

8

Mail carriers follow a route.

They drop off mail.

They also pick up the mail

people send.

Some mail carriers walk.
They carry mail in a bag
or cart.

Why might some mail carriers walk?

Other mail carriers have a mail truck.

They drive to each mailbox.

Each mail carrier wears a uniform.

He wears a hat.

He wears comfy shoes too.

Mail carriers work in all kinds

of weather.

This mail carrier works in the snow!

Mail carriers work hard.

They work long hours.

They bring people their mail every day.

Mail Carrier Tools

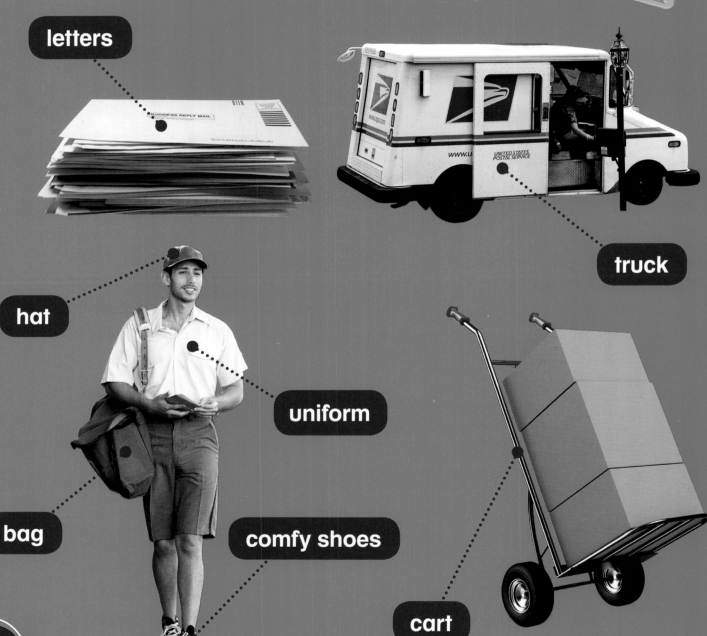

letters

truck

hat

uniform

bag

comfy shoes

cart

Picture Glossary

communities

groups of people who live in the same area

route

the usual way people go to get somewhere or do something

sort

to group similar things together

uniform

a special set of clothes worn for work

23

Read More

Christopher, Nick. *What Do Mail Carriers Do?* New York: PowerKids Press, 2016.

Meister, Cari. *Mail Carriers*. Minneapolis: Jump!, 2014.

Murray, Julie. *Mail Carriers*. Minneapolis: Abdo Kids, 2016.

Index

Photo Credits